BENJAMIN BRITTEN

Three Character Pieces

(1930)

for piano

FABER _ff_ MUSIC

The first public performance of the *Three Character Pieces*
was given by Sarah Briggs at St. Mary's Centre, Chester,
on 28 July 1989 as part of the Chester
Summer Music Festival

Duration: c. 9 minutes

© 1989 by Faber Music Ltd
First published in 1989 by Faber Music Ltd
3 Queen Square London WC1N 3AU
Cover design by M & S Tucker
Printed in England

The title page of the composition sketch (in the Britten-Pears Library at Aldeburgh) is headed 'Three Pieces for Pianoforte', with the names of the dedicatees – or perhaps more accurately, the friends pictured within – underneath: 1. John 2. Daphne 3. Michael. These were three young friends of Britten's – John Boyd, Daphne Black and Michael Tyler. Britten's diary entries do not reveal a great deal about the origins of the pieces, although his characteristically disparaging remarks include, à propos of No. 3, 'It is terribly hard & I simply haven't the technique.'

Apparently, Britten did not make a fair copy of the work, and, although he may have played the pieces privately, there is no record of a public performance. The absence of a fair copy has inevitably meant closer editorial attention than is usually necessary in the case of Britten's juvenilia, and, since parts of the pencil manuscript were evidently written rather hastily, a number of conjectural readings have had to be made.

One unresolved problem is the C (natural) at the top of the phrase in bar 48 of No. 1, followed by a C flat in bar 50. This may well have been an intentional difference; but discrepancies between the opening and the 'recapitulation' of No. 3 have been removed, since they are almost certainly due to Britten's hasty copying of the earlier section.

The three pieces are dated respectively September 16th, October 14th and December 17th 1930. The passage in quotation marks on p.15 is from John Ireland's 'Ragamuffin' (No. 2 of *Three London Pieces*, published in 1918), and was no doubt intended as a small homage to his composition teacher at the Royal College of Music, where Britten had just completed his first term. But the music owes more to his previous teacher, Frank Bridge, and it is surely due to him that these three pieces, hardly characteristic of Britten, are stylistically closer to Ravel and Scriabin than to the mainstream of English music in the 1930s.

C.M.

Three Character Pieces
(1930)

Benjamin Britten
(1913-1976)

1. **Poco allegro vivace**

September 16th 1930

6

2. Poco andante grazioso

October 4th 1930

3. Poco presto e molto capriccioso

a tempo al fine

December 27th 1930